# FRANCIS FRITH'S
# REDDITCH
## LIVING MEMORIES

**JULIE ROYLE** was born in Cheshire and grew up there and in Northumbria. She studied history at the University of Exeter because she wanted to live in the West Country. She now lives near Worcester, in a small country cottage with a large unruly garden, and works as a freelance photographer and writer specialising in landscape, wildlife, travel, conservation, environmental issues and local history. She has a passion for Africa, which she has visited many times, but loves Britain too, particularly the English Lake District.

**FRANCIS FRITH'S**
**PHOTOGRAPHIC MEMORIES**

# REDDITCH
## LIVING MEMORIES

### JULIE ROYLE

First published in the United Kingdom in 2004 by
Frith Book Company Ltd

Limited Hardback Subscribers Edition 2004
ISBN 1-85937-800-5

Paperback Edition 2004
ISBN 1-85937-521-9

British Library Cataloguing in Publication Data

Redditch Living Memories
Julie Royle

Frith Book Company Ltd
Frith's Barn, Teffont,
Salisbury, Wiltshire SP3 5QP
Tel: +44 (0) 1722 716 376
Email: info@francisfrith.co.uk
www.francisfrith.co.uk

Printed and bound in Great Britain

Front Cover: **REDDITCH,** *Alcester Street c1960* R840041A
Frontispiece: **HANBURY,** *Hanbury Wharf c1965* H501003

*The colour-tinting is for illustrative purposes only, and is not intended to be
historically accurate*

AS WITH ANY HISTORICAL DATABASE THE FRITH ARCHIVE IS CONSTANTLY
BEING CORRECTED AND IMPROVED, AND THE PUBLISHERS WOULD
WELCOME INFORMATION ON OMISSIONS OR INACCURACIES

# CONTENTS

# FRANCIS FRITH
## VICTORIAN PIONEER

FRANCIS FRITH, founder of the world-famous photographic archive, was a complex and multi-talented man. A devout Quaker and a highly successful Victorian businessman, he was philosophical by nature and pioneering in outlook.

By 1855 he had already established a wholesale grocery business in Liverpool, and sold it for the astonishing sum of £200,000, which is the equivalent today of over £15,000,000. Now a very rich man, he was able to indulge his passion for travel. As a child he had pored over travel books written by early explorers, and his fancy and imagination had been stirred by family holidays to the sublime mountain regions of Wales and Scotland. 'What lands of spirit-stirring and enriching scenes and places!' he had written. He was to return to these scenes of grandeur in later years to 'recapture the thousands of vivid and tender memories', but with a different purpose. Now in his thirties, and captivated by the new science of photography, Frith set out on a series of pioneering journeys up the Nile and to the Near East that occupied him from 1856 unti 1860.

**INTRIGUE AND EXPLORATION**

These far-flung journeys were packed with intrigue and adventure. In his life story, written when he was sixty-three, Frith tells of being held captive by bandits, and of fighting 'an awful midnight battle to the very point of surrender with a deadly pack of hungry, wild dogs'. Wearing flowing Arab costume, Frith arrived at Akaba by camel sixty years before Lawrence of Arabia, where he encountered 'desert princes and rival sheikhs, blazing with jewel-hilted swords'.

He was the first photographer to venture beyond the sixth cataract of the Nile. Africa was still the mysterious 'Dark Continent', and Stanley and Livingstone's historic meeting was a decade into the future. The conditions for picture taking confound belief. He laboured for hours in his wicker dark-room in the sweltering heat of the desert, while the volatile chemicals fizzed dangerously in their trays. Back in London he exhibited his photographs and was 'rapturously cheered' by members of the Royal Society. His reputation as a photographer was made overnight.

**VENTURE OF A LIFE-TIME**

Characteristically, Frith quickly spotted the opportunity to create a new business as a specialist publisher of photographs. He lived in an era of immense and sometimes violent change. For the poor in the early part of Victoria's reign work was exhausting and the hours long, and people had precious little free time to enjoy themselves. Most people had no transport other than a cart or gig at their disposal, and rarely

business one only has to look at the catalogue issued by Frith & Co in 1886: it runs to some 670 pages, listing not only many thousands of views of the British Isles but also many photographs of most European countries, and China, Japan, the USA and Canada - note the sample page shown on page 9 from the hand-written Frith & Co ledgers recording the pictures. By 1890 Frith had created the greatest specialist photographic publishing company in the world, with over 2,000 sales outlets - more than the combined number that Boots and WH Smith have today! The picture on the next page shows the Frith & Co display board at Ingleton in the Yorkshire Dales (left of window). Beautifully constructed with a mahogany frame and gilt inserts, it could display up to a dozen local scenes.

travelled far beyond the boundaries of their own town or village. However, by the 1870s the railways had threaded their way across the country, and Bank Holidays and half-day Saturdays had been made obligatory by Act of Parliament. All of a sudden the working man and his family were able to enjoy days out and see a little more of the world.

With typical business acumen, Francis Frith fore-saw that these new tourists would enjoy having souvenirs to commemorate their days out. In 1860 he married Mary Ann Rosling and set out on a new career: his aim was to photograph every city, town and village in Britain. For the next thirty years he travelled the country by train and by pony and trap, producing fine photographs of seaside resorts and beauty spots that were keenly bought by millions of Victorians. These prints were painstakingly pasted into family albums and pored over during the dark nights of winter, rekindling precious memories of summer excursions.

### THE RISE OF FRITH & CO

Frith's studio was soon supplying retail shops all over the country. To meet the demand he gathered about him a small team of photographers, and published the work of independent artist-photographers of the calibre of Roger Fenton and Francis Bedford. In order to gain some understanding of the scale of Frith's

### POSTCARD BONANZA

The ever-popular holiday postcard we know today took many years to develop. In 1870 the Post Office issued the first plain cards, with a pre-printed stamp on one face. In 1894 they allowed other publishers' cards to be sent through the mail with an attached adhesive halfpenny stamp. Demand grew rapidly, and in 1895 a new size of postcard was permitted called the court card, but there was little room for illustration. In 1899, a year after Frith's death, a new card measuring 5.5 x 3.5 inches became the standard format, but it was not until 1902 that the divided back came into being, so that the address and message could be on one face and a full-size illustration on the other. Frith & Co were in the vanguard of postcard development: Frith's sons Eustace and Cyril continued their father's monumental task, expanding the number of views offered to the public and recording more and more places in Britain, as the coasts and countryside were opened up to mass travel.

Francis Frith had died in 1898 at his villa in Cannes, his great project still growing. The archive he created continued in business for another seventy years. By 1970 it contained over a third of a million pictures showing 7,000 British towns and villages.

## FRANCIS FRITH'S LEGACY

*Frith's legacy to us today is of immense significance and value, for the magnificent archive of evocative photographs he created provides a unique record of change in the cities, towns and villages throughout Britain over a century and more. Frith and his fellow studio photographers revisited locations many times down the years to update their views, compiling for us an enthralling and colourful pageant of British life and character.*

*We are fortunate that Frith was dedicated to recording the minutiae of everyday life. For it is this sheer wealth of visual data, the painstaking chronicle of changes in dress, transport, street layouts, buildings, housing, engineering and landscape that captivates us so much today. His remarkable images offer us a powerful link with the past and with the lives of our ancestors.*

## THE VALUE OF THE ARCHIVE TODAY

*Computers have now made it possible for Frith's many thousands of images to be accessed almost instantly. Frith's images are increasingly used as visual resources, by social historians, by researchers into genealogy and ancestry, by architects and town planners, and by teachers involved in local history projects.*

*In addition, the archive offers every one of us an opportunity to examine the places where we and our families have lived and worked down the years. Highly successful in Frith's own era, the archive is now, a century and more on, entering a new phase of popularity. Historians consider the Francis Frith Collection to be of prime national importance. It is the only archive of its kind remaining in private ownership. Francis Frith's archive is now housed in an historic timber barn in the beautiful village of Teffont in Wiltshire. Its founder would not recognize the archive office as it is today. In place of the many thousands of dusty boxes containing glass plate negatives and an all-pervading odour of photographic chemicals, there are now ranks of computer screens. He would be amazed to watch his images travelling round the world at unimaginable speeds through internet lines.*

*The archive's future is both bright and exciting. Francis Frith, with his unshakeable belief in making photographs available to the greatest number of people, would undoubtedly approve of what is being done today with his lifetime's work. His photographs depicting our shared past are now bringing pleasure and enlightenment to millions around the world a century and more after his death.*

# REDDITCH
## AN INTRODUCTION

**REDDITCH IS** located in the north-east corner of Worcestershire, on the Warwickshire border 16 miles south of Birmingham. It was designated a New Town in 1964 to house Birmingham overspill and to alleviate overcrowding in the West Midlands conurbation. But it is not entirely urban: around half of the borough of Redditch is rural, with hilly countryside and attractive villages such as Feckenham.

A New Town it may be, but Redditch is not so very new, though it did develop later than other Worcestershire towns. Two prehistoric trackways pass through the borough, and there is an earthwork at Beoley which may just possibly be an Iron Age fort, but there is no real evidence of any settlement at this time. A Roman road, Ryknield (or Icknield) Street, runs through the neighbourhoods of Washford, Matchborough, Ipsley and Church Hill; but it bypasses the town centre by a couple of miles, and there is no evidence of

**BARNT GREEN,** *Lower Bittell Reservoir c1965* B417009

Roman settlement in Redditch. Local placenames often end in -ley (for instance Batchley, Beoley, Bordesley, Bridley, Ipsley and Studley), which indicates that they were Saxon settlements, based on clearings in the Forest of Feckenham (another Saxon name), made from the sixth century onwards. Despite this, there is no proof of any settlement on the site of the present-day town centre until Bordesley Abbey was founded by Cistercian monks in 1138.

The monks owned huge estates on which they raised sheep, and they soon grew rich from the wool trade. They were also skilled engineers: they diverted the River Arrow, built an extensive drainage system, created fish ponds and harnessed water power to drive a corn mill and two other mills used for industrial purposes. One of these was probably on the site of Forge Mill, which is now a museum dedicated to the needle industry. Exactly when a lay settlement began to develop alongside the abbey is unclear, but the monks would have required a workforce, and we know that by 1248 a hamlet called Rededitch or

Red-dyche was in existence. It is said to have taken its name from Batchley Brook, which runs through a layer of water-staining red marl.

After initially flourishing, Bordesley Abbey suffered various setbacks, most notably the Black Death in 1348. It never fully recovered; but the end did not come until 1538, with Henry VIII's Dissolution of the Monasteries. The abbey was dismantled, the monks were pensioned off and most of the lay community moved to higher, drier ground where the modern town now stands. Only the abbey's gatehouse chapel survived intact, and the people of Redditch continued to use it until 1805, when it was demolished. Since 1969, comprehensive and continuing excavations have revealed much of the monastic floor plan, as well as many artefacts and skeletons.

Redditch's main claim to fame is not Bordesley Abbey, but the humble needle. For many years Redditch was pre-eminent in the industry of needle manufacture, which first came to England in the late 1550s, introduced to London by Flemish immigrants. In the 1640s needle making was

**FECKENHAM,** *The Square c1960*  F65006

becoming established in Studley and Sambourne, where it was based on the cottage system. As it flourished it spread to other localities, reaching Alcester in 1670 and Redditch in the early 1700s. By the 1770s it was the main employer in Redditch, which was still a village at that time.

The first documented needle makers in the town were the Sherward brothers in the early 18th century, but more famous names include Henry Milward and Abel Morrall. Water power was an important factor in the development of the industry: corn mills on the River Arrow were converted into needle mills, though many of the processes were carried out in the workers' homes. It was only in the early 19th century that a steam-powered factory system was developed. At its peak, in the mid 19th century, a staggering 90% of the world's needles were made in Redditch, and the quality of the product was deemed second to none. Even today, there are still craftspeople the world over who will use only Redditch-made needles for their work.

It is believed that in the 1850s up to 100 million needles were made every week in and around Redditch. Needles come in many different types, with domestic needles falling into hundreds of categories, and medical needles into thousands. Industrial usage of needles is varied too, from saddle making to space-age requirements - Redditch needles were used to attach heat-resistant tiles to

**REDDITCH,** *St Stephen's Parish Church c1955* R84024

the space shuttle Columbia, for instance. Despite the diversity of the product, it would have been dangerous to be totally reliant on the needle industry. Fortunately, Redditch was never in that position, and by the early 19th century the fishing tackle trade had also become hugely important. The manufacture of fish hooks began in Redditch around 1770, and by 1880 Samuel Allcock & Company was the world's largest manufacturer of fishing tackle.

The third most important local industry was spring making, which began in Redditch in the mid-19th century, its origins closely linked to the needle and fish hook trades. The most prominent manufacturer was Herbert Terry & Sons Ltd. Established in 1855, Terrys specialised at first in artificial bait, and then moved on to other precision metalware, including springs. As the cycle and car industries expanded, so did the range of goods demanded from companies such as Terrys. War was good for business too, and Terrys supplied pins for hand grenades and valve springs for the engines of Spitfires and Hurricanes. By the middle of the 20th century, Terrys was producing an enormous range of products; it still trades in Redditch, though the involvement of the Terry family ceased in 1975 soon after the company was taken over.

Redditch's population growth was rapid in the 19th century. From the 1840s onwards it became increasingly built up, and in 1894 it was made an Urban District. Its industrial base saw further

**STUDLEY,** *The Manor House c1960* S299017A

diversification. Royal Enfield, the manufacturer of cycles and motor bikes, was just one important new local company. This rapid expansion during the 19th century was followed by slower but steady growth throughout the 20th century. Between 1929 and 1933 Ipsley, Feckenham, Crabbs Cross, Astwood Bank and parts of Alvechurch and Webheath were taken into Redditch. New housing estates were built at Batchley, Mayfields, Abbeydale and Studley Road. By 1964 the largest single employer was the metal manufacturing industry, followed by the engineering and spring trades, with needles and fishing tackle now some way behind, though still highly regarded in terms of quality. Needles are still made today in Studley, where Needle Industries turns out around 400 million a year.

In 1964 the population was around 32,000, and Redditch was poised on the brink of a new era. Its designation that year as a New Town began a period of enormous change, the most dramatic in the town's history. By the time the Redditch Development Corporation was wound down in

1985, the population had doubled in size and thousands of new homes had been built, together with millions of square feet of industrial and office space. A new road network had been imposed, and the town centre had been redeveloped to include a huge mall, the Kingfisher Shopping Centre.

The town was planned as a series of 'neighbourhoods', each with about 10,000 people. Houses were grouped around a local centre providing essential services, while industrial areas, schools and other facilities were built nearby. The neighbourhoods are linked by footpaths and by regular buses and bounded by perimeter roads linking with dual carriageways carrying through traffic. The footpaths are provided with footbridges and subways to ensure that pedestrians and cars are well segregated.

It looks good on paper, but it is not universally popular. Even before the controversial New Town status was acquired, Redditch provoked conflicting opinions. Walter Savage Landor, writing in 1830, claimed there never was 'an habitation

**WILMCOTE,** *The Crofts c1955* W216003

14

more thoroughly odious', but for Alexander Hay Japp in 1877 it was 'a very clean and beautiful little town'. Views are similarly polarised today. Redditch is now a large town which has consumed far more countryside than could really be spared. The new estates were built between 1968 and 1981 - dates which tell us all we need to know about the building styles employed. The Kingfisher Centre is of the same vintage, opening in phases between 1973 and 1981. The interior is pleasant enough in the usual bland sort of way, but the exterior, with its multi-storey car parks, is of surpassing ugliness.

There was much opposition to the New Town development, and many local people old enough to remember Redditch as it was will never be reconciled to what has happened. Others, especially some of those who moved into the area from the West Midlands conurbation, think it a fine place to live and work. It is now the second largest town in the county, having overtaken old-established market centres such as Bromsgrove, Kidderminster and Evesham, all of which have been in existence longer than Redditch.

One of the most striking things for the first-time visitor to Redditch is the abundance of greenery, and the great thing about it is that it is mostly native greenery, not the usual inappropriate municipal planting. Only small fragments of the original woodland survive, such as Pitcheroak, Foxlydiate and Oakenshaw woods, but they are authentic fragments, survivors rather than interlopers (though some non-native species have been introduced), and bursting with bluebells in the spring. In addition to the existing woods, over two million trees were planted, most of them native species, as part of the massive landscaping project undertaken by the Development Corporation. Redditch also contains areas of low-lying wet meadowland, the most exciting of which is Ipsley Alders, a peat fen with rushes and sedges - an extremely rare habitat in the West Midlands.

The design of the new development was intended to create a feeling of wide open spaces with landscaped housing estates integrated into the environment. Opinions differ as to how

**BROMSGROVE,** *High Street 1949* B233006

successfully this was achieved, but there is certainly plenty of green space. The massive Arrow Valley Country Park runs through the heart of the borough, incorporating woods, meadows, a large lake with sports and leisure facilities, and a fair amount of wildlife too. On the northern side of the park the excavated ruins of Bordesley Abbey can be seen in Abbey Meadows, and the adjacent Forge Mill Museum features the only surviving water-driven needle mill in the world.

The new road system (all 90 miles of it) looks overwhelming when viewed on a map, but in real life one is pleasantly surprised by the hedgerows and copses which soften the blow, many of them retained from former farmland rather than newly planted. Traffic is effectively segregated, with housing areas linked to local facilities and to the town centre by a network of footpaths and underpasses. All in all, when we look at certain other New Towns, we realise that there are plenty of worse places to live than Redditch. Indeed, much of it is very pleasant, by any standards. On the other hand, nothing can excuse the demolition of so much of the Victorian town to make way for the Kingfisher Centre.

**REDDITCH,** *Evesham Street c1955* R84039

# REDDITCH TOWN CENTRE

**REDDITCH,** *St Stephen's Parish Church c1955*
R84024

St Stephen's stands on the Green, around which people first settled when they moved from Bordesley after the Dissolution of the Monasteries. Church Green is still, in many ways, the focal point of the redeveloped town.

**REDDITCH,** *St Stephen's Parish Church c1965* R84056

In 1855 St Stephen's replaced the Chapel on the Green, built in 1805 to replace the ancient chapel at Bordesley. The architect was Henry Woodyer of Guildford, but his rather uninspiring Decorated-style church was substantially restored and extended in 1893-94 by Temple Moore.

**REDDITCH,** *St Stephen's Parish Church c1950*  R84001

The local sandstone is not that durable, and St Stephen's has needed more than one restoration in the course of its relatively short life. On one such occasion, in 1905-06, it is said that the town librarian, Mr Lewis, took advantage of the scaffolding to climb to the top of the spire. Dragging a cumbersome plate camera with him, he took four photographs, looking north, south, east and west.

▼ **REDDITCH,** *Church Green c1950* R84015

Many of the trees on the Green were planted in the 1850s, when prosperous locals were invited to plant a tree for the hefty sum of £5 each. Church Green remains a popular place to relax on sunny days, as the woman in this photograph is doing.

▶ **REDDITCH**
*The Fountain,*
*Church Green c1955*
R84016a

This ornamental cast-iron fountain is an entertaining affair painted in cream and green and featuring some lifelike crested cormorants (or shags) beneath a statue of a woman believed to represent Temperance. It was cast at Coalbrookdale in 1883, and presented by the Bartleet family to mark the provision of mains water to the town.

◀ **REDDITCH**
*Church Green c1950*
R84016

The modern Alexandra Hospital is some distance from the town centre, but the building visible through the trees on Church Green in this view is Smallwood Hospital, paid for by the needle makers Edwin and William Smallwood in 1895. It still houses clinics and other medical facilities.

▶ **REDDITCH**
*Market Place c1960*
R84040

Market Place lost its market in 1949. Fortunately, it has since been pedestrianised and the market restored. Blue-and-white and green-and-white striped awnings cover the rows of stalls which threaten to overflow into the churchyard.

**REDDITCH**
*Market Place c1955*
R84027

The market originally took place on the Green, but was confined to the south side of it after the Chapel on the Green was built in 1805. It was only then that this street became known as Market Place. In 1949 the market was moved to Red Lion Street, but it is now back on two sides of the Green - Market Place and Church Green East.

▼ **REDDITCH,** *Huins Shoes, Market Place c1955* R84027a

Huins Shoes dominated the corner of Market Place for over half a century, but it has gone now, and a bakery occupies the premises. James Huins also had shops in Evesham, Northfield and King's Norton, but the main branch was here at Redditch, along with the head office. It was advertised rather grandly as Boot Metropole.

▶ **REDDITCH**
*Market Place c1965*
R84044

This picture shows the new Woolworth's which replaced the small one seen in R84044a (page 25). Next to Woolworth's is Currys, which opened in about 1934, selling bicycles in those days, as well as the electrical goods we associate with it now.

◄ **REDDITCH**
*Market Place c1950*
R84012

There are familiar names here, with Barclays Bank, Woolworth's, Currys, Freeman Hardy Willis and Hepworths. None of them remains on the same site, though Woolworth's has not moved far. The small, white-painted Woolworth's store in this picture was demolished, along with part of its handsome neighbour, to make way for a larger Woolworth's in the 1960s.

► **REDDITCH**
*Woolworth's,*
*Market Place c1960*
R84044a

Tony's Handyman Centre has occupied this site since Woolworth's moved into the Kingfisher Centre over 20 years ago. Currys, next door, is now occupied by a building society. Today Currys trades from an edge-of-town superstore in St Georges.

**REDDITCH**
*Alcester Street 1949*
R84013

Most of Alcester Street was
demolished in the 1960s, but
this small part of it survived.
The building to the left of
the prominent awning was
Watkins' Tea Rooms at the
beginning of the 20th
century, and the gable end
(the northern one, not visible
in this photograph) still
carries the painted legend
'luncheon, dining, tea rooms'
and also advertises
accommodation for cyclists.

▶ **REDDITCH**
*Evesham Street c1950*
R84007

Promotional material published about Redditch tells us that the existing town centre was 're-planned', an innocuous-sounding word which, in this context, really means 'destroyed'. In this 1950s street scene only one building has been spoilt, and that could have been restored. Instead, almost the entire street was demolished to accommodate the Kingfisher Centre. Only two or three buildings on the left of this picture survive.

◀ **REDDITCH**
*Alcester Street c1960*
R84041a

This detail from R84041 (page 29) brings the Palace Theatre into more prominence. Although it still survives, it no longer looks quite the same; a box-shaped extension was added to it in the 1970s, replacing its attractive three-storey brick-built neighbour.

◄ **REDDITCH**
*Alcester Street c1960*
R84041

All the foreground buildings were demolished in the 1960s. In fact, only two buildings in this scene are still intact today; one is the church, and the other is the Palace Theatre (the light-coloured structure behind the cyclist). A new town hall now stands opposite the Palace, while the foreground area has been sacrificed to the road system.

**REDDITCH**
*Evesham Street c1950*  R84008

This view is almost identical to
R84007 (page 28), but the
photographer has stepped back to
include Huins on Market Place
corner and its neighbours,
E A Hodges and Boots the Chemist.
E A Hodges had been there at least
50 years at the time of the
photograph. It was a stationer's,
but was described as a 'fancy
repository' in early advertisements.

**REDDITCH**
*Evesham Street c1955*
R84026

Boots is not shy of advertising itself - no less than four signs are visible here, two of them huge. 'Boots for developing and printing' proclaims the banner overhanging the street - no doubt it took a little longer than the one-hour service Boots offers today.

**REDDITCH,** *Evesham Street c1955* R84039

Earlier pictures of Evesham Street show Cranmore Simmons on the corner, a family-run furniture business established by Alfred Simmons in the 1920s. Here we can see its replacement, a Burton's store typical of 1950s building styles (one hesitates to call it architecture). This was one of the few Evesham Street buildings to survive the demolitions of the 1960s (to the dismay of many - little did they know that even worse was still to come). Today it houses the Yorkshire Bank and Provident Personal Credit.

**REDDITCH**
*Evesham Street c1960*
R84042

E A Hodges, the long-established, family-run stationery and news store, remained a well-known presence in town at this time. It still published and sold a great many picture postcards, though perhaps not so cheaply as at the beginning of the century when it used to advertise an album of 12 postcards for one shilling (five pence).

**REDDITCH,** *Evesham Street c1967* R84057

This must have been taken very shortly before work began on the demolition of Evesham Street. E A Hodges has become just another branch of Dillons, presumably as a result of a take-over. Boots has updated its fascia again (see R84026 page 32 and R84042, above), while still retaining, as it does to this day, the traditional script.

**REDDITCH**
*Evesham Street c1965*
R84054

None of these buildings survived the 1960s. The one with the clock was Hopkins, a jeweller's shop, but in the early 20th century it had been Liptons, one of the first chain grocers, a forerunner of today's supermarkets. On the left of the picture is The Talbot, built in 1926 on the site of an earlier inn, The Vine.

**REDDITCH,** *Evesham Street c1955* R84037

This is the south end of Evesham Street, but none of this survives. Anybody standing today in approximately the same position as the photographer would see nothing more than a couple of dreary buildings and one of the Kingfisher Centre's multi-storey car parks.

**REDDITCH,** *A Newsagent and Post Office, Evesham Street c1955* R84037a

This detail from R84037 (page 34) is a reminder of how our streets were once filled with a profusion of tobacco advertisements - Capstan, Player's, St Julien, St Bruno, Gold Flake, Senior Service - hardly any famous brand of the time is missing. The lad outside the shop is wearing a sleeveless jumper, very characteristic of the period, and a more informal version of the buttoned waistcoat worn by the elderly man on the left.

**REDDITCH**
*The Parade, Church Green West c1950* R84011

This is one part of Redditch which has not greatly changed, although the traffic is a great deal heavier now. Few would dare to venture onto the roads in the vulnerable contraption driven by the man on the right.

▶ **REDDITCH**
*The Parade, Church Green West c1955*
R84025

Hardly anybody refers to Church Green West as the Parade anymore, and it is unlikely that many recall an even earlier time when it was sometimes known as the Promenade. But a few do still refer to Hepworths Corner, even though Hepworths went from this site long ago.

◀ **REDDITCH**
*The Parade, Church Green West c1950*
R84009

The handsome building in the centre of this view, adorned with a balustrade and pinnacles, was a branch of the Midland Bank in 1950. A branch of HSBC, which swallowed up Midland some years ago, now stands on the same site but not in the same building. Its replacement is a grey structure shaped like a shoebox, but with far less charm.

▲ **REDDITCH,** *The Parade, Church Green West c1950* R84010

Buckley's, in the centre here, is still recognisable, although the lettering on the end wall has been removed and the awnings have gone. The ground floor now features a plastic fascia, and ugly steel blinds protect the windows when the shops which occupy the building are closed.

◀ **REDDITCH**
*The Parade, Church Green West c1960*
R84043b

The lime trees which grace Church Green West no longer have the lollipop shape seen here. They look even more unnatural these days, as they are severely pollarded in the French style, but they would be much missed if they were removed.

**REDDITCH**
*The Parade, Church
Green West c1960*
R84043a

The Gas Service building on the right housed the offices and showroom of Redditch Gas Company at the time of this photograph. It had been built about 30 years earlier on the site of a demolished Victorian building. While it has escaped a similar fate itself, it has been greatly altered to fit the corporate style of MacDonald's.

**REDDITCH,** *The Parade c1950*  R84017

The building on the right was erected in 1922 to house the Redditch Benefit Building Society (founded in 1859). It seems slightly ironic, given that the purpose of building societies was to enable people to own their own homes, that an attractive cottage was demolished to make way for this rather grandiose structure.

### REDDITCH
*The Redditch Benefit Building Society c1950* R84017a

This detail from R84017 (page 40) provides a close-up view of the former home of the Redditch Benefit Building Society. It is now Birmingham Midshires, and has been much modernised, though it is just about recognisable. Church Green West has become a street of building societies, with West Bromwich and Nationwide (in the former Hepworths Corner) at the other end.

**REDDITCH,** *Bates Hill Methodist Church c1955*  R84022

This imposing and quite enormous Wesleyan chapel is testimony to the power of Methodism in 19th-century Redditch. It was opened in 1843, and was extended in 1881; but it was demolished in the 1980s to make way for a gas and electrical superstore. Fortunately, the foreground trees have matured well and screen the new building quite effectively.

# SOME REDDITCH NEIGHBOURHOODS

**REDDITCH**
*The Garden of Remembrance c1955* R84019

Green-painted iron gates inscribed 'In memory of the fallen' open into the Garden of Remembrance from Plymouth Road, just round the corner from the bus station. The cenotaph does not look quite so pristine these days: the plaque is missing, and the niche containing the eternal flame is guarded on both sides by ugly plastic panels.

**REDDITCH**
*The Garden of Remembrance c1955*
R84020

Many of the flowering plants enjoying the sun in this picture have been replaced by low-maintenance shrubs, including too many gloomy evergreens. A dark spine of conifers runs down the middle of the long garden, which is just a narrow strip of land between Plymouth Road and the cemetery.

**REDDITCH,** *The Garden of Remembrance c1960*  R84047

Visitors to the garden will look in vain for this children's playground today, though we can still see where it was. The house behind the hedge has gone too.

▶ **REDDITCH**
*The County High
School and the
Playing Fields c1950*
R84005

Opened in 1929, the
County High later
became Abbey High
and then, in 2002,
Trinity High. It stands
in extensive grounds
just off Easemore
Road, an easy walk
from several Redditch
neighbourhoods and
from the bus and
train stations. A Sixth
Form Centre shares
the same site.

◀ **REDDITCH**
*The County High
School c1955* R84028

The first school in
Redditch was built in
1820 on land donated by
a local landowner, the
Earl of Plymouth, at the
junction of Unicorn Hill
and Bates Hill. However, it
was not until 1909 that
Redditch acquired its first
secondary school. Like
the later County High, it
was on Easemore Road.
Much extended, it now
serves as a college.

◀ **REDDITCH**
*The County High School
c1955* R84029

These covered passageways look almost like an updated version of cathedral cloisters, in the much plainer style of the 20th century. It is amazing to think that it was only as recently as 1844 that an Education Act required local authorities to provide secondary schools for all.

**REDDITCH**
*Batchley Estate c1955*
R84036

This was farmland until 1933, when 210 houses were built. The estate was greatly enlarged in the 1940s and 1950s when a further 1050 houses were added. It looks rather tired today, but the houses were well-built and substantial, with gardens and green space all around. It is easy to forget, with the good living conditions that so many of us enjoy today, that such things were often a novelty in the 1950s.

▶ **REDDITCH**
*Batchley Lakes, the Estate
c1955* R84035

The lake provides a focal
point for Batchley Estate,
and has acquired a fringe of
vegetation since 1955.
Children enjoy watching the
resident Canada geese,
mallard ducks and
moorhens, while a local
angling club meets here
every Wednesday.

◀ **REDDITCH**
*Bridley Moor High School*
*c1955* R84034

Redditch was slow to provide educational facilities in the first half of the 20th century. After the passage of the 1944 Education Act, steps were taken to remedy the situation; Bridley Moor Secondary Modern (as it then was) opened in 1952, the first purpose-built secondary school for those who failed to make it to the high school.

**REDDITCH**
*The Abbey Stadium
Sports Centre c1965*
R84059

Land allocated for woodland, open space, golf courses and sports facilities accounts for nearly a quarter of the New Town area. The Abbey Stadium has been much extended since 1965, to include a large sports hall and a multi-gym.

**REDDITCH,** *The Abbey Stadium Sports Ground c1965* R84060

As well as indoor facilities (see R84059, above), an athletics track, tennis courts, soccer pitches and a bowling green are all available at the sports centre, which occupies a semi-rural site not far from the ruins of Bordesley Abbey.

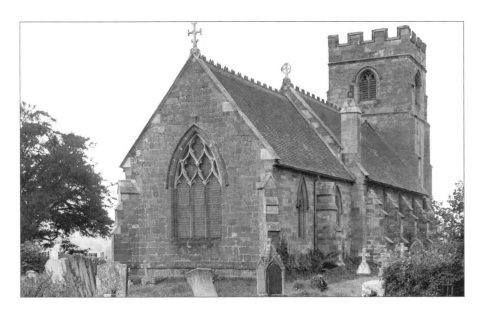

**REDDITCH**
*St Peter's Church,
Ipsley c1955* R84023

Ipsley was in Warwickshire when it was mentioned in *Domesday Book* (1086), and only transferred to Worcestershire in 1931. It predates Redditch, but has long since been swallowed up by it. St Peter's was built in 1345, probably on the site of a Saxon church. Next to it stands Ipsley Court, where the poet Walter Savage Landor (1775-1864) lived as a boy.

**BEOLEY,** *Main Road c1965* B845003

Beoley predates Redditch, but it remains a small village on the northern edge of the present New Town. In 1140 the Norman Lord of the Manor, Geoffrey of Limesey, built a church (probably on the site of a Saxon one) dedicated to St Leonard, patron saint of prisoners and, appropriately enough, of iron workers.

▼ **BEOLEY,** *The Village Inn c1965* B845001

In the early 20th century, when Beoley was still completely rural, The Village Inn used to be a popular destination for people venturing out of town by horse-drawn carriage or by bicycle. The car park was a garden then, and many thousands of afternoon teas were served there to townsfolk over the years.

▶ **REDDITCH**
*The Star and Garter, Crabbs Cross c1965*
R84049

Changed, but still recognisable, The Star and Garter presides over a major road junction constantly busy with traffic. It was notorious in the 19th century for the activities which Redditch men got up to in the field behind the pub. Bull baiting, bare-knuckle boxing and cock fighting all took place, often watched by up to 500 men.

◄ **REDDITCH**
*Evesham Road,*
*Crabbs Cross c1965*
R84048

In May 1643 King Charles I, raising troops for war, reviewed 10,000 men at 'Crabbe Crosse' - or so it is said. It seems a large number if they were drawn only from the local area. Crabbs Cross mushroomed in the 19th century as rural needle makers moved into the area to be nearer the new Redditch factories.

▶ **ASTWOOD BANK**
*Evesham Road c1965*
A163350

Redditch town centre occupies high ground near the northern end of the prehistoric Ridgeway. Astwood Bank developed in linear fashion along the Ridgeway, which is now the main road to Pershore and Evesham. The Bell Inn has been providing refreshment for travellers for centuries and is today little changed from this picture, though Whitbread is now the name on the sign.

**ASTWOOD BANK**
*Evesham Road c1965*
A163012

This stretch of Evesham Road has hardly changed, except for the constant traffic. The bus shelter outside The White Lion (left) has gone, but this is still one of the main stops for Redditch-bound buses (The Bell - see A163350 on page 53 - is another). The house with the timbered gable stands just north of an ancient junction where Evesham Road (the prehistoric Ridgeway) meets Feckenham Road and Sambourne Lane.

**▶ ASTWOOD BANK**
*Western Hill Close*
*c1965* A163353

A wide range of architectural periods is represented in Astwood Bank, though Victorian buildings are particularly numerous. The 1960s brought a number of new developments, of which this is typical. It had probably only just been completed in 1965 - the gardens are obviously newly planted.

**◀ ASTWOOD BANK**
*The Park c1965* A163352

All those families moving into Astwood Bank's new houses in the 1960s needed facilities, and the community does have a fair range. The park seems to have been popular then, but is less so today. Maybe the constant traffic on neighbouring Evesham Road puts people off.

▲ **ASTWOOD BANK,** *The Parish Church c1965* A163005

The Church of St Matthias and St George was built in 1884 and enlarged in 1911, with the works carried out by Huxleys, a local building company. Unlike most churches, it has no tower to mark its position, and few people passing through Astwood Bank will even realise it has a church.

◄ **ASTWOOD BANK**
*Green Sleeves c1965*
A163006

Three stages of construction can be seen here, with the central section probably the oldest. The insubstantial timbers in the right-hand wing were probably plastered over originally. Very often, an enthusiasm for imagined 'authenticity' leads to timbers being revealed which were never meant to be.

# WARWICKSHIRE VILLAGES

**SAMBOURNE,** *The Green Dragon c1965* S600002

The village lies south of Redditch, with Studley and Astwood Bank encroaching from east and west. Sambourne was one of the earliest centres of the needle industry, but it never grew to any great size. Today, altered and extended 17th-century buildings, such as The Green Dragon, mingle with modern suburban houses.

58

**STUDLEY**
*Studley College c1960*
S299017d

Designed in 1834 by the architect Beazley, this bizarre Gothic Revival structure was from 1903 until the 1960s the home of Studley College, founded by Frances, Countess of Warwick. Her aim was the instruction of women in various branches of agriculture. Financial problems eventually forced its closure, and British Leyland bought it to use as a marketing centre.

**STUDLEY,** *The Old Castle c1960* S299017b

This group of buildings next to the church was built in the 16th century on the site of a medieval castle. Traces of the motte and the moat are still visible in the garden. The house sits in fields beside the River Arrow, away from the built-up part of Studley.

**TANWORTH-IN-ARDEN,**
*The Village c1965* T124009

The character of the village has changed greatly in recent years as commuters have discovered it. Modern houses surround it now, but the heart of the original village is the Green, with its chestnut tree, Georgian houses and The Bell Inn, still bedecked with flowers as in this picture.

**TANWORTH-IN-ARDEN,** *The Village c1965* T124010

Little remains today of Shakespeare's Forest of Arden, only isolated islands of woodland in a sea of agriculture. But the name lives on locally. Unlike the more famous Henley-in-Arden, however, Tanworth received its suffix quite recently, in an attempt to put an end to confusion with Tamworth (Staffordshire).

**ULLENHALL,** *The Village c1955* U19004

The Winged Spur (in the background, on the right) in the village
centre is still a traditional country pub with a warm welcome for
local residents and visitors. Like so many villages, however,
Ullenhall has lost its shops, post office, school and vicarage.

▶ **ULLENHALL**
*The Perry Mill c1955*
U19003

Perry is a similar drink to cider, but is made from pears instead of apples. It has traditionally been associated more with Worcestershire than Warwickshire, but even in Worcestershire it is hard to find these days, with just a handful of small producers still making it.

◀ **ULLENHALL**
*The White Cottage and the Memorial c1965*  U19008

Ullenhall has had its share of notorious residents, including a 19th-century forger called William Booth, who was also accused of his brother's murder. Though acquitted of that charge he was hanged anyway, for forgery was a capital offence. Another infamous resident was Lady Luxborough, whose husband hid her away there in 1736 because she had been scandalising London. She still managed to upset strait-laced locals by her antics at her house, Barrells Park, which lies in ruins after a fire in 1933 and is said to be haunted by her ghost.

## WILMCOTE

*Mary Arden's House c1965* W216127

This beautiful farmhouse near Stratford was built in the 16th century. It was in 1789 that it was first given the name of Mary Arden's House, reflecting a local tradition that it had been the home of Shakespeare's mother before her marriage. The house was acquired by the Shakespeare Birthplace Trust in 1930 and furnished as it would have been in Mary's day. Millions of tourists have visited it since. It was only very recently that it was discovered that it had never been Mary Arden's house after all - she had lived next door at Glebe Farm. Fortunately, that also belonged to the Shakespeare Birthplace Trust and was already open to visitors, promoted as a historic farm with a Victorian interior.

▶ **WILMCOTE**
*The Swan Guest House*
*c1955* W216009

The Shakespeare properties are not the only impressive buildings in Wilmcote. The Swan is a handsome structure which looks as if it might originally have been a farmhouse. Nowadays it is The Swan House Inn.

◄ **WILMCOTE**
*The Green and the Swan
Guest House c1955*
W216008

With all those pilgrims coming to visit what they thought was Mary Arden's house, it was obviously necessary for Wilmcote to provide refreshments and accommodation, and The Swan did just that. The majority of tourists these days visit only briefly, often covering the whole of 'Shakespeare Country' in one day.

▶ **WILMCOTE**
*The Crofts c1955*
W216003

Warwickshire's vernacular architecture characteristically uses a mixture of building materials; with stone in the Cotswolds, for instance, and an abundance of timber in the formerly well-wooded areas of Arden. But Wilmcote was a quarrying centre, and this timber-framed house has a garden wall of the local lias limestone.

# WORCESTERSHIRE VILLAGES

**FECKENHAM,** *High Street c1960* F65007

From Saxon times Feckenham was the administrative centre for the Forest of Feckenham, which once covered most of north Worcestershire. In fact, Feckenham was virtually a town when Redditch was barely even a village. Today, Feckenham is only a village, but a large, prosperous one with fine houses and charming cottages, many of them formerly inhabited by needle makers who worked at home.

69

**FECKENHAM**
*The Square c1960*
F65006

Some of the best houses in Feckenham are clustered around the village green, or the Square, though only glimpses are revealed here. The village has houses from most periods, but is most notable for its Georgian ones and for several truly magnificent timber-framed farmhouses in the surrounding countryside.

**FECKENHAM,** *Droitwich Road c1960* F65010

Droitwich has a long history of salt production. The Romans mined Droitwich salt on a large scale, and this is the road they built running east from Droitwich through Feckenham to Alcester. It is still known as the Saltway, though it was only one of several saltways which radiated out in all directions from Droitwich.

### FECKENHAM
*Alcester Road c1960*
F65009

It is interesting to note that the brick cottages in the centre have a timber-framed gable end, revealing a much older origin than the brickwork suggests. The dormer windows in the roof, giving additional light and space to the first floor, were probably inserted at the same time as the brick facade was added.

**HANBURY,** *The Post Office c1965* H501013

Hanbury sprawls along the B4091, which runs north from the Saltway to Bromsgrove. This view shows the junction of the two roads, where The Vernon Arms has been offering refreshment to travellers for many years. It takes its name from the Vernon family who lived at Hanbury Hall, a Wren-style mansion built in 1701 and given to the National Trust in 1953.

▼ **HANBURY,** *The Parish Church c1965* H501006

St Mary's Church has a prominent hilltop position with views to the Malverns and the Cotswolds. It was delightfully but fancifully described by the 17th-century historian Habington as 'invironed with highe and mighty trees and able to terrifye a far-off ignorant enimy with a deceitful showe of an invincible castell.' He was obviously influenced by the local tradition (for which there is no evidence) that an Iron Age fort once occupied the hilltop. The church is of 12th-century origin, but was rebuilt in the late 18th century.

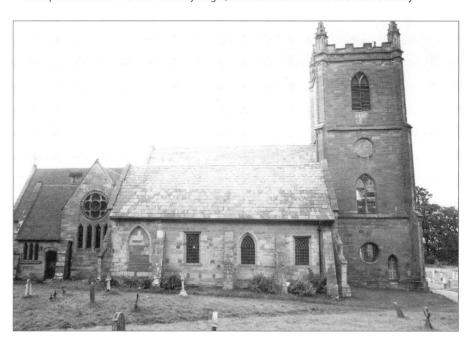

▶ **HANBURY**
*Dodderhill Common c1965*
H501007

Also known as Piper's Hill Common, this beautiful nature reserve has developed from wood pasture; that is, rough grazing with a scattering of trees. Grazing ceased about 150 years ago, and generations of self-seeded saplings have since created mature woodland. It is one of only a handful of woods of this type in the West Midlands. It is also unusual (in this region) in being composed mainly of beech trees, though there are other species too, notably oak and sweet chestnut. Naturalists describe very old trees as 'veteran', and there are over 250 veteran trees here, some possibly 300-400 years old.

◄ **HANBURY**
*Hanbury Wharf c1965*
H501003

The wharf is closer to Droitwich than Hanbury, next to the place where the Worcester and Birmingham Canal (opened 1815) is joined by the Droitwich Junction Canal. This opened in 1854, making it one of the last canals to be built. It linked with the Droitwich Barge Canal to connect the town and its salt trade to the River Severn via the Worcester and Birmingham Canal. It had become derelict by the 1930s, but Droitwich Canals Trust has restored some sections, including the top pound at Hanbury Wharf.

► **HANBURY**
*The Gate Hangs Well c1965* H501010

The Gate, as locals call it, is at Woodgate, by a crossroads in a pleasant rural location between Hanbury and Bromsgrove. The origin of its unusual name is obscure. There is a pub of the same name in Redditch situated on a former turnpike road, and it is believed to have taken its name from the turnpike gate, but that is unlikely to be the case here.

# BROMSGROVE AND THE LICKEYS

**BROMSGROVE,** *Aerial View c1955* B233039

Bromsgrove lies a few miles west of Redditch, and it is an ancient market town which has become a suburban satellite of Birmingham. This aerial shot shows the High Street; it is a wonderful illustration of a common style of urban development, with narrow medieval burgage plots running back at right angles from the road. These were infilled with houses and courts as the town grew and pressure on land increased. Development, particularly road building, has destroyed this pattern in Bromsgrove.

**BROMSGROVE**
*High Street 1949* B233006

The High Street was still predominantly Georgian at this time. On the right-hand side is The Golden Cross Hotel, rebuilt in 1932 on the site of one of Bromsgrove's oldest coaching inns. When the railway opened in 1840 a horse bus took passengers from The Golden Cross to the station at Aston Fields. A bell was rung to let passengers know when the bus was ready to go.

► **BROMSGROVE**
*High Street c1960*
B233046

This section of the High Street is now pedestrianised, but the east side of the street is not greatly changed from this view. Timothy Whites is still a handsome building, though it is W H Smith now. Pre-1950s pictures of the High Street show several timber-framed buildings, but most had gone by 1960.

◄ **BROMSGROVE**
*High Street c1965* B233057

This lovely building is at the southern end of the High Street, in the former market place where the High Street meets Worcester Road and St John's Street. The scaffolding is there because the rest of the building has just been pulled down. Photographs taken before 1965 reveal it to have been a truly magnificent structure; documentary records indicate that it was built about 1600, though its predecessors can be tracked back as far as 1460. Together with the surviving building, it was known as Appleby's Corner, after the ironmonger who occupied it for many years.

▲ **BROMSGROVE,** *High Street into St John's Street c1965* B233090

The scaffolding visible in B233057 (page 78) has been replaced by this 1960s box, hardly a worthy successor to Appleby's Corner. It is hard to imagine a more incongruous pairing than these two, both of which are now occupied by solicitors. The fine house in the background survives unspoilt today, and is also used as solicitors' offices.

◄ **BROMSGROVE**
*The Church and the Council House c1955*
B233032

This scene remains virtually unchanged today, but it has been cut off from the High Street by an ugly ring road. The Council House is now called St John's Court, and is occupied by the Somerset Redstone Trust. The Church of St John the Baptist is of Norman origin; its spire is visible for many miles around.

**BARNT GREEN**
*Fiery Hill Road c1965*
B417007

Barnt Green Station (hidden behind the trees) is on the Birmingham-Gloucester line, which opened in 1840. In 1844 an omnibus service was provided to take people the five miles or so from Redditch to Barnt Green Station, and it was only in 1859 that Redditch's first station opened - and even then the line ran only to Barnt Green.

**BARNT GREEN,** *Fiery Hill Road c1965*  B417003

A local landowner, the Earl of Plymouth, encouraged the building of Barnt Green Station (on the left here) for the convenience of his tenant farmers. It was only in the 1880s, however, when much of the Plymouth estate was sold off, that development began. Houses were built near the station, and a recognisable village centre began to form, with a range of amenities.

**BARNT GREEN**
*The Green c1965*
B417001

Barnt Green was essentially a purpose-built village for rail commuters and therefore Victorian in style. Some of its early character remains, but there has also been considerable later development, typical of which are the houses glimpsed here.

**BARNT GREEN,** *Bittell Lane c1965* B417010

On the eastern edge of Barnt Green, Bittell Lane is built up, but the houses are set in fairly large gardens and there is still almost a semi-rural feel. The two Bittell Reservoirs, the Worcester and Birmingham Canal and some pleasant countryside are all just a short stroll away for the lane's residents.

▶ **BARNT GREEN**
*Lower Bittell
Reservoir c1965*
B417009

When the Worcester
and Birmingham
Canal was
constructed, it was
taken across the
watershed of the
River Arrow, which
meant a loss of
headwater for the
Arrow. Lower Bittell
Reservoir was built to
compensate mill
owners for this loss.

◀ **LICKEY**
*The Bittell Reservoirs
c1965* L215021

It is difficult to pinpoint
the viewpoint (possibly
Bilberry Hill) and to be
sure which reservoirs we
are looking at here. The
foreground one is
possibly Cofton Reservoir
and the other may be
Upper Bittell Reservoir,
which was built as a
canal feeder in 1836.

◀ **REDNAL**
*View of Lickey Hills c1965*
R250014

This view is from Groveley Lane, looking towards Four Ways at Rednal, where the black and white pub just visible was then The Chalet Club, and now The Poacher's Pocket. This has always been considered the gateway to the Lickeys for visitors from Birmingham.

▶ **REDNAL**
*The Old Rose and Crown c1965* R250013

The Old Rose and Crown is near the bottom of Rose Hill, a former Roman road which later formed part of the Birmingham-Bristol road; it became a toll road in 1726. In 1758 a regular stagecoach service was established between Birmingham and Worcester, with The Rose and Crown a popular stop en route. When a new road with easier gradients was opened through Rubery in 1831, the Rose Hill route was no longer used by coaches and The New Rose and Crown opened at Rubery. The Rose and Crown at Rednal became The Old Rose and Crown.

**LICKEY**
*The Woods c1965* L215018

This view could be Cofton Woods, Pinfield Wood or Lickey Warren, among others. In the Middle Ages the whole area was densely wooded with patches of heathland and small clearings for agriculture and settlement. It was Royal Forest for a time, but it was confirmed as common land by Edward I. However, just as the railway in 1840 opened up the Lickeys to day trippers, local landowners were enclosing land to keep the public out. The Birmingham Association for the Preservation of Open Spaces was formed to fight against encroachment, and Birmingham Corporation gradually acquired much of the area, partly through donations from the Cadburys. Eventually, almost the whole of the wooded area of the Lickeys was preserved for the public.

## LICKEY
*The Post Office c1965*  L215009

Lickey village is an unremarkable sort of place, but the name is famous among railway buffs because the two-mile Lickey Incline (between Bromsgrove and Barnt Green) is, almost incredibly, the steepest stretch of mainline railway in Britain. In the days of steam, at least one extra banking engine (often more) was required to push each train up the Lickey. The most famous of the bankers was Big Bertha, which clocked up 800,000 miles on the Lickey between 1920 and 1956. Even in a modern train, the change in gear is obvious as it tackles the incline.

**LICKEY,** *The Church c1965* L215016

Holy Trinity Church was built in 1856, designed by Henry Day in the Early English style. Close by stands Lickey Grange, the former home of Lord Austin (1866-1941), who founded the nearby Longbridge car factory in 1905. The renowned Austin Seven was designed in the billiard room at Lickey Grange by Austin himself and Stanley Edge.

# INDEX

# NAMES OF SUBSCRIBERS

The following people have kindly supported this book by subscribing to copies before publication.

Roger P. Amor
Maurice & Doris Askew, Redditch & New Zealand
The Bennett Family
John W. Borland, Studley
The Bott Family, Redditch
The Bough & Adams Families, Redditch
The Bourne Family, Redditch
In Memory of C. M. Bowers, Redditch
Mr & Mrs G. P. Brookes and 'Carlo'
The Brough Family, Redditch
In Memory of Mrs Wendy Anne Cook
The Curtis Family, Redditch
Ursula Murray Cutts, Redditch
Mr. A. S. & Mrs. R. M. Daniels, Studley
Hazel & Eric Dent
Mr P. J. & Mrs R. N. Ellins, Redditch
Mr H. & Mrs J. Evans, Redditch
In Memory of Vera Farron, Redditch
In Memory of Mary & Des Faulkner
N. Ferris, Studley
W. Ferris, Redditch
J. A. & M. E. Finney, Studley
Jennifer Eileen Forman, Redditch
The Foster Family, Redditch
Anthony B. Freeman, Studley
Mrs V. Gibbs, Redditch
Mona Griffin & Zillah Harris, Astwood Bank
In Memory of Fred & Gwen Hicks, Redditch
Ronnie Hill, Diane Hill & Mrs Walker
The Don Hughes Family, Redditch
Donald Humphries, Abbots Mortons
Humphries Shoe Shop, Redditch
David Johnson, Redditch
Alan Jones, Headless Cross
Judy & Brad, Kingston, Ont., Canada
In Memory of Heather Jukes, Redditch
In Memory of John Kilgallen, Redditch
Ian Lamb, Redditch
Lorraine Latham & Daniel Latham

Peter & Jane Leahy
The Lealand Family, Redditch
Dedicated to my darling wife Linda
Lynne & Pete, St Stephen's Grange, Redditch
Geoff & Lynda Mee, Redditch
Phil, Phillipa & Ciaran Mee, Harrogate
In memory of Jack & Gladys Moore of Crabbs Cross, Redditch
F. Harvey Morris
To Mum love from Lynette
Trevor & Maxine Nall (formerly Eaves) Redditch
For the Newell and Skidmore Families, Redditch
Mr A. D. Niland, Studley
The Noon Family, Redditch
In Loving Memory of Eliza Onions & Dolly Harper
The Onions Family, Redditch
The Parkes Family, Redditch
Mr D. J. & Mrs M. M. Parsons, Redditch
Mr & Mrs L. Peak
To Penny on her 18th Birthday love Suzie & Peter
Margaret Pratt on your 70th Birthday
The Preece Family, Studley
David Read
Matthew Ryder, Redditch
Brian Sadler, 70th Birthday 14th April 2004
The Sayers Family, Redditch
Mr. V. W. Shorey
The Springthorpe Family, Redditch
John P. Stroud, Redditch
Derrick L. Steward
Mick Steward Happy 56th Birthday love from Marion x
Happy Birthday to Derek Taylor love Jan & Ian
Laurence & Gail Teague
Mr Vernon Walton, Redditch
Brian Frank Warner, a Redditch man and proud of it, with love A.N.
In Memory of Desmond Henry Westbury 1926-1979
The Wheatcroft Family, Redditch
In Memory of Dad & Mum, Fred & Ruth Wiggett, Redditch
The Wiggett Family, Redditch
Mrs Monica Wood, Redditch
Mrs P Wood
Mr A. & Mrs M. M. Wright

# FRITH PRODUCTS & SERVICES

Francis Frith would doubtless be pleased to know that the pioneering publishing venture he started in 1860 still continues today. Over a hundred and forty years later, The Francis Frith Collection continues in the same innovative tradition and is now one of the foremost publishers of vintage photographs in the world. Some of the current activities include:

## Interior Decoration

Today Frith's photographs can be seen framed and as giant wall murals in thousands of pubs, restaurants, hotels, banks, retail stores and other public buildings throughout the country. In every case they enhance the unique local atmosphere of the places they depict and provide reminders of gentler days in an increasingly busy and frenetic world.

## Product Promotions

Frith products are used by many major companies to promote the sales of their own products or to reinforce their own history and heritage. Frith promotions have been used by Hovis bread, Courage beers, Scots Porage Oats, Colman's mustard, Cadbury's foods, Mellow Birds coffee, Dunhill pipe tobacco, Guinness, and Bulmer's Cider.

## Genealogy and Family History

As the interest in family history and roots grows world-wide, more and more people are turning to Frith's photographs of Great Britain for images of the towns, villages and streets where their ancestors lived; and, of course, photographs of the churches and chapels where their ancestors were christened, married and buried are an essential part of every genealogy tree and family album.

## Frith Products

All Frith photographs are available Framed or just as Mounted Prints and Posters (size 23 x 16 inches). These may be ordered from the address below. From time to time other products - Address Books, Calendars, Table Mats, etc - are available.

## The Internet

Already fifty thousand Frith photographs can be viewed and purchased on the internet through the Frith websites and a myriad of partner sites.

For more detailed information on Frith companies and products, look at these sites:

www.francisfrith.co.uk
www.francisfrith.com
*(for North American visitors)*

---

See the complete list of Frith Books at:
*www.francisfrith.co.uk*

This web site is regularly updated with the latest list of publications from the Frith Book Company. If you wish to buy books relating to another part of the country that your local bookshop does not stock, you may purchase on-line.

---

*For further information, trade, or author enquiries please contact us at the address below:*
**The Francis Frith Collection, Frith's Barn, Teffont, Salisbury, Wiltshire, England SP3 5QP.**
Tel: +44 (0)1722 716 376  Fax: +44 (0)1722 716 881  Email: sales@francisfrith.co.uk

# See Frith books on the internet at www.francisfrith.co.uk

# FREE MOUNTED PRINT

**Mounted Print**
*Overall size 14 x 11 inches*

**Fill in and cut out this voucher and return**
*it with your remittance for £2.25 (to cover postage and handling). Offer valid for delivery to UK addresses only.*

**Choose any photograph included in this book.**
*Your SEPIA print will be A4 in size. It will be mounted in a cream mount with a burgundy rule line (overall size 14 x 11 inches).*

**Order additional Mounted Prints at HALF PRICE (only £7.49 each*)**
If you would like to order more Frith prints from this book, possibly as gifts for friends and family, you can buy them at half price (with no additional postage and handling costs).

**Have your Mounted Prints framed**
For an extra £14.95 per print* you can have your mounted print(s) framed in an elegant polished wood and gilt moulding, overall size 16 x 13 inches (no additional postage and handling required).

---

**\* IMPORTANT!**

**These special prices are only available if you order at the same time as you order your free mounted print. You must use the ORIGINAL VOUCHER on this page (no copies permitted). We can only despatch to one address.**

---

*Send completed Voucher form to:*
**The Francis Frith Collection, Frith's Barn, Teffont, Salisbury, Wiltshire SP3 5QP**

# Voucher *for **FREE** and Reduced Price Frith Prints*

*Please do not photocopy this voucher. Only the original is valid, so please fill it in, cut it out and return it to us with your order.*

| Picture ref no | Page no | Qty | Mounted @ £7.49 | Framed + £14.95 | Total Cost |
|---|---|---|---|---|---|
| | | 1 | Free of charge* | £ | £ |
| | | | £7.49 | £ | £ |
| | | | £7.49 | £ | £ |
| | | | £7.49 | £ | £ |
| | | | £7.49 | £ | £ |
| | | | £7.49 | £ | £ |

*Please allow 28 days for delivery*

| | |
|---|---|
| * Post & handling (UK) | £2.25 |
| **Total Order Cost** | £ |

Title of this book . . . . . . . . . . . . . . . . . . . . . . . . . . .

I enclose a cheque/postal order for £ . . . . . . . . . .
made payable to 'The Francis Frith Collection'

OR please debit my Mastercard / Visa / Switch / Amex card
*(credit cards please on all overseas orders)*, details below

Card Number

Issue No (Switch only)          Valid from (Amex/Switch)

Expires          Signature

Name  Mr/Mrs/Ms . . . . . . . . . . . . . . . . . . . . . . . . . . .

Address . . . . . . . . . . . . . . . . . . . . . . . . . . . . . . . . . . .

. . . . . . . . . . . . . . . . . . . . . . . . . . . . . . . . . . . . . . . . .

. . . . . . . . . . . . . . . . . . . . . . . . . . . . . . . . . . . . . . . . .

. . . . . . . . . . . . . . . . . . . . . . . . . . . Postcode . . . . . . . . .

Daytime Tel No . . . . . . . . . . . . . . . . . . . . . . . . . . . .

Email . . . . . . . . . . . . . . . . . . . . . . . . . . . . . . . . . . . .

Valid to 31/12/05

**Would you like to find out more about Francis Frith?**

We have recently recruited some entertaining speakers who are happy to visit local groups, clubs and societies to give an illustrated talk documenting Frith's travels and photographs. If you are a member of such a group and are interested in hosting a presentation, we would love to hear from you.

Our speakers bring with them a small selection of our local town and county books, together with sample prints. They are happy to take orders. A small proportion of the order value is donated to the group who have hosted the presentation. The talks are therefore an excellent way of fundraising for small groups and societies.

**Can you help us with information about any of the Frith photographs in this book?**

We are gradually compiling an historical record for each of the photographs in the Frith archive. It is always fascinating to find out the names of the people shown in the pictures, as well as insights into the shops, buildings and other features depicted.

If you recognize anyone in the photographs in this book, or if you have information not already included in the author's caption, do let us know. We would love to hear from you, and will try to publish it in future books or articles.

**Our production team**

Frith books are produced by a small dedicated team at offices in the converted Grade II listed 18th-century barn at Teffont near Salisbury, illustrated above. Most have worked with the Frith Collection for many years. All have in common one quality: they have a passion for the Frith Collection. The team is constantly expanding, but currently includes:

Jason Buck, John Buck, Douglas Mitchell-Burns, Ruth Butler, Heather Crisp, Isobel Hall, Julian Hight, Peter Horne, James Kinnear, Karen Kinnear, Tina Leary, David Marsh, Sue Molloy, Kate Rotondetto, Dean Scource, Eliza Sackett, Terence Sackett, Sandra Sampson, Adrian Sanders, Sandra Sanger, Julia Skinner, Lewis Taylor, Shelley Tolcher and Lorraine Tuck.